A WELCOME FOR YOUR CHILD

A Guide to Baptism for Parents

JULIE KAVANAGH &
MAEVE MAHON

VERITAS

First published 2008 by
Veritas Publications
7/8 Lower Abbey Street
Dublin 1
Ireland
Email publications@veritas.ie
Website www.veritas.ie

ISBN 978 1 84730 088 1

Designed by Colette Dower
Cover photograph by Thomas Sunderland Photography, © Diocese of
Kildare & Leighlin
Illustrations by Mary Cawley
Printed in the Republic of Ireland by Betaprint Ltd, Dublin

CONTENTS

ACKNOWLEDGEMENTS

We wish to thank the following for their support in the course of writing this book: Bishop Jim Moriarty, Fr Bill Kemmy and our fellow team members in the Kildare & Leighlin Faith Development Services.

A special word of thanks to Larry and Orla McHugh for giving us permission to use the image on the front cover.

PREPARING FOR BAPTISM

THINGS TO THINK ABOUT AND DO

A key element of any significant celebration in our lives is preparation. Baptism is one such significant moment. It marks the beginning of your child's journey of faith. You need to spend time preparing for the church celebration. There are a number of areas that will need your consideration.

Why do I want my Child Baptised?

This is a key question for the parents of any child to be presented for baptism. The decision to baptise a child carries with it responsibilities that will last long after the celebration is over. Baptism is much more than a way of naming and welcoming your child into the world: it is the beginning of their journey of faith. It is the first step in becoming a life-long member of the church. Baptism is a sacrament, a graced moment in which we meet God, and the decision to celebrate this sacrament deserves careful consideration.

Notification to the Parish

You will need to notify your parish well in advance of your wish to baptise your child. This may involve a call to your priest or to the parish office. Many parishes now have set times for baptisms, perhaps once or twice a month, usually on a Saturday or Sunday. If this is not the case the decision as to the most appropriate time can be made in consultation with the parish representative.

Parish Preparation

There are many different kinds of parish preparation on offer throughout the country. The purpose of all preparation is to allow parents become familiar with the baptism ceremony and have some conversation about the meaning of baptism. There may also be an opportunity for becoming more actively involved in the baptism celebration, such as choosing and reading the scripture passages, writing and reading the Intercessions. In some situations parish baptism teams visit the homes of the child to be baptised. Others may require attendance at a baptismal preparation meeting held at a central location in the parish. Many parishes provide parents with a publication such as this one to help them to get ready at home. The initial contact with the parish will clarify what is required.

CHOOSING GODPARENTS

A Word about Godparents

As parents you may have decided already who the godparents of your child will be. Or you may be at the point of considering who to ask. Either way, it is helpful to know what exactly the role of a godparent is in the eyes of the Church and what specific requirements there are for a godparent. The custom of having two godparents, one of each sex, seems to be a fairly established practice – while it is perfectly acceptable to have just a godmother or a godfather.

Your child's godparents are required to be members of the Catholic Church and to have celebrated all three sacraments of initiation – Baptism, Confirmation, Eucharist. There is the further requirement that they must be living a life consistent with faith – given their role as a godparent. Quite simply this means that they must be seeking to live a life informed by their Catholic faith – with all the struggles that that entails. A godparent is not a super-Catholic! But hopefully a godparent is someone who is comfortable with their Catholic identity and is willing to support parents who are handing on this faith to their child.

Obviously the responsibility of being a godparent is one that requires a level of maturity. In the Catholic Church a person of sixteen years is deemed to have reached this level and therefore a godparent is someone who is sixteen years or older.

At the request of the parents, a baptised and believing Christian, not belonging to the Catholic Church, may also act as a Christian witness along with a Catholic godparent.

So in considering who you ask to be godparents to your child the above needs to be taken into account. You are asking the godparents of your child to support you as you hand on faith. In order to help godparents to understand this, you might share this section and the final section of the book with them.

BAPTISMAL CANDLE

You will need a baptismal candle for your child. These can be bought from religious shops or from many stationary shops. If you have older children they might like to help make a special baptismal candle by decorating a plain white candle with symbols such as water, a dove and cross. Keep the candle somewhere safe after the baptism. It could be lit on your child's birthday and perhaps on the anniversary of their baptism. It will probably be needed when they continue their journey of initiation in celebrating the Sacraments of Confirmation and First Holy Communion.

WHITE GARMENT

Many families have a tradition of passing a christening robe or baptismal gown from one generation to the next, a very visible sign of the handing on of faith. Sometimes this robe is handmade. If your family has not had this kind of tradition perhaps you could start it for your generation.

Today most babies are brought to the church in their white baptismal clothes. The reasons for this are obvious and probably very practical. However, it may be possible to retrieve some of the wonder of the clothing with the white garment. Some parishes suggest that the child be wrapped in a coloured blanket or shawl until this moment of the ceremony. They are then revealed in all their beauty. It is also possible to dress your child in a simple one piece until this point in the ceremony and then slip the robe over their head and show them as a new creation to all those gathered.

ON THE DAY

Arrive at the church in plenty of time to meet the priest or baptismal team member. Encourage family members to be on time also. This will give you plenty of time to become familiar with the surroundings and ensure that everyone is able to have a couple of moments of quiet reflection before the ceremony begins. This is a sacred and special time, and it is important to be conscious of this during the ceremony.

REGISTRATION OF BAPTISM

When your child has been baptised their name will be entered in the parish baptismal register. Normally the name will be recorded in exactly the same form as on the civil register, which is on your child's birth certificate. Some parishes will require a copy of the birth certificate in order to enter the information. The priest will confirm all such details with you before completing the entry in the parish's baptismal register. The practice of giving copies of baptismal certificates to parents differs from parish to parish. If you do not receive a copy of the certificate either on the day or shortly afterwards it is important to keep a record of the date of your child's baptism. You may be asked to provide a baptismal certificate when your child begins school or when they come to celebrate other sacraments.

OVERVIEW OF THE RITE

Reception of the Children
Greeting
Opening Dialogue
Signing of the Children with the Cross
Invitation to the Celebration of the Word of God

Liturgy of the Word
Readings
Homily
Intercessions

Preparatory Rites
Prayer of Exorcism
Anointing before baptism

Celebration of Baptism
Invitation to Prayer
Prayer over the Water
Profession of Faith
Renunciation of Sin
Profession of Faith
Baptism
Acclamation

Explanatory Rites
Anointing after Baptism
Clothing with White Garment
Lighted Candle
Ephphetha

Concluding Rite
Lord's Prayer
Blessing and Dismissal

The baptism of a child is a very special occasion in the life of a family. It is also a very special occasion in the life of the Church. Just as you welcome this little one into your family, so too, the Church welcomes your child into the family of God. Your child is loved by God and is a welcome addition to the Christian family. Baptism celebrates this love and welcome of your child.

In the course of the celebration of baptism, you will experience a rich tapestry of symbols, actions, gestures, prayers and the Word of God. All these elements work together to try to communicate something of the deep meaning of baptism for your child, your family and the wider Christian community. This book is intended to help families understand more fully what is being expressed through the various parts of the baptism ceremony.

We hope that this book will also help parents, godparents and the whole family to know that they have a real contribution to make to the ceremony. Baptism, like all liturgy, is something that we do together.

As can be seen from the outline of the Rite of Baptism, the celebration follows a very definite path. As the sacrament of welcome into the life of the Church, it begins with 'The Reception of the Children'. Here the children being presented for baptism are first formally welcomed into the Christian family. In some parishes this takes place at the actual door of the Church – the place where we normally greet people into our homes.

The children, their families and the presiding priest or deacon then join the rest of the gathered assembly in the main body of the Church to participate in the Liturgy of the Word. The Word of God is central to our Christian faith. In the years to come this word will be a source of on-going nourishment for your child as they grow in faith. The readings are explained in the homily and then we respond in prayer. Finally in this part of the ritual we remember the saints who have gone before us – those who witness for us what it means to be followers of Christ.

The 'Prayer of Exorcism' and the 'Anointing Before Baptism' that follow are described as Preparatory Rites. They represent the final moments of preparation before baptism takes place. These final moments are characterised by praying for your child and the other children being presented for baptism, and by physically anointing each of them on the breast with blessed oil. We pray that they will be strengthened with the power of Christ.

It is now time to move to the font – the fountain of our new life in Christ – for the Celebration of Baptism. Here, water is blessed in a prayer that reminds us of the powerful way in which God has and continues to act in our lives and throughout all of human history. Here, you, as a parent, and the godparents you have chosen for your child renounce sin and profess your faith. Having received your profession of faith, the Church, in the person of the priest or deacon, is ready to respond to your request to have your child baptised in the faith of the Church. In the name of the Trinity, our God who is Father, Son and Holy Spirit, your child is then baptised.

The Explanatory Rites that follow seek to do just that – to explain further the deep meaning of baptism. Through the accompanying prayers and the ritual gestures of the anointing after baptism, the clothing with the white garment, the handing over of the lighted candle and the touching of ears and mouth we approach something of the mystery, invitation and gift of baptism.

The final stage of our celebration brings us to the altar. Baptism is the gateway through which your child enters to become a member of the Christian family. The celebration of Confirmation and Eucharist will mark their full membership into the life of the Church. The Eucharist will sustain them in their Christian life-long journey. Now, gathered around the altar, in the Concluding Rite we pray the Lord's Prayer, as children of God. Aware of our need for God in the reality of our lives, our final action in the celebration of Baptism is to seek

God's blessing upon us. And then we are dismissed, sent out in peace, together with our children, the newest members of the family of God.

In the pages that follow you will find both the Rite of Baptism itself and an explanation of the Rite. The text of the Rite is found on the left hand pages while the right hand side contains the related explanation.

THE RITE

AT THE DOOR

Reception of the Children

Greeting
The celebrant greets all present, and especially the parents and godparents, reminding them briefly of the joy with which the parents welcomed their children as gifts from God, the source of life, who now wishes to bestow his own life on these little ones.

EXPLANATION OF THE RITE

AT THE DOOR

Reception of the Children

The Rite of Baptism begins with the reception of the children, during which the children are publicly named; the parents ask for baptism, godparents declare their support and the children receive the sign of the cross as a gesture of welcome by the Church. The sign of the cross reminds us that God is with us in every moment of our lives – God's love reaches beyond the depth and width of our experience. Our relationship with God is central to who we are as human beings.

Greeting

The first moments of the Rite of Baptism are marked by a sense of welcome. Your child and the other children being presented for baptism are waiting to take their place among the Christian faithful. In this celebration they are being formally and publicly welcomed into the family of God. This is a great moment in the life of the Church whose membership will be enriched for years to come by the presence of these children. The joy that you as parents felt in welcoming your child into the world is now felt by the Christian community as it welcomes these children, these gifts from God.

It is in this spirit of joy that the welcome at the beginning of this Rite of Baptism extends beyond the children, to their parents, families and friends.

Opening Dialogue

First the celebrant questions the parents of each child.

Celebrant

What name do you give your child?

Parents

Name

Celebrant

What do you ask of God's Church for N.?

Parents

Baptism.

Opening Dialogue
In the opening dialogue you will be asked three central questions – the name you are giving your child; what you are asking of the Church for your child; and your willingness to accept responsibility for raising your child in the practice of their faith.

Naming
This may be the first time your child is named publicly. To share this name out loud is a powerful thing. This is the name you chose for your child. This is the name they will carry with them. This is the name you whisper at night time to sooth them to sleep and it is the name with which you welcome them to a new day. This name is now who they are.

In the Bible the giving of a name is often connected to being called by God. We find God giving Abram the name Abraham and telling Abraham that he will have a son whom he is to call Isaac. We find the angel Gabriel telling Mary that she will bear a son whom she is to name Jesus. Time and time again in the Bible we hear God calling people by their name. And God continues to call us each by name. We are not anonymous. Each of us has a place with God. Your child is a child of God, called by God.

The name you have chosen for your child is of significance. There is a widely held tradition of choosing the name of a saint as one of the children's names. The saints provide us with models of Christian living. By choosing a saint's name you can also hope that your children will try to live up to their example. Of course, sometimes we might find ourselves naming our children after the 'unofficial saints' that we have met in our lives.

What you are asking of the Church
As a parent you have brought your child to the church to celebrate baptism. At the beginning of the celebration you have an opportunity to state out loud, in front of family, friends and members of the community of faith your wishes from the Church for your child.

Before the day of baptism this question might be useful to reflect upon as a parent. For the years to come, what are your hopes for your child as a member of the Church? What do you ask of God's Church for your child? As an adult member of this same Church, how will you help the Church in meeting these hopes for your child?

Celebrant
You have asked to have your children baptised. In doing so you
are accepting the responsibility of training them in the practice of
faith. It will be your duty to bring them up to keep God's
commandments as Christ taught us, by loving God and our
neighbour? Do you clearly understand what you are undertaking?

Parents
We do.

Then the celebrant turns to the godparents and addresses them in
these or similar words:
Are you ready to help these parents in their duty as Christian
mothers and fathers?

All the godparents
We are.

Signing of the Children with the Cross
The celebrant continues:

Name and Name the Christian community welcomes you with
great joy.
In its name I claim you for Christ our Saviour by the sign of his
cross.
I now trace the cross on your foreheads, and invite your parents
(and godparents) to do the same.

He signs each child on the forehead, in silence. Then he invites the
parents and the godparents to do the same.

Accepting Responsibility
As a parent, you are reminded that by asking to have your child baptised you are also recognising certain responsibilities that belong to you. Just as any parent is expected to look after the emotional and physical needs of their children, so too as a parent it is your responsibility to nurture the faith life of your children. While you will hopefully have the support of parish and school in the years to come, faith grows in the home above all else. The home will be the most important place where your child will learn and discover the Christian virtues of faith, love and hope, as experienced in your family.

Support of Godparents
The primary role of godparents is one of support. They do not take over the Christian duties of a parent but are there to offer you help and support as you seek to build a Christian home for yourself and your family. In the ceremony they publicly give this support. In many ways, they are present not just as family members or friends but as representatives of the wider Christian community.

Signing of the Children with the Cross
The words of the priest speak of the joy of the Christian community at this new member in their midst. The sign of the cross that accompanies these words is the sign that marks us all as Christians. This is the first time your child is publicly marked by this sign – a sign of blessing and promise, a sign of belonging to Christ and the Christian family. This familiar gesture of our faith is made by the priest, who then invites the parents and godparents to do the same. This is a sign that you can continue to share with your child at home and one that hopefully they will experience as a constant part of their life.

At the Ambo

The Liturgy of the Word

Readings and Homily

Readings

One or even two of the following gospel passages are read, during which all may sit if convenient.

John 3:1-6	The meeting with Nicodemus
Matthew 28:18-20	The apostles are sent to preach the gospel and to baptise
Mark 1:9-11	The baptism of Jesus
Mark 10:13-16	Let the little children come to me

Between the readings, responsorial psalms or verses may be sung. The texts of these readings can be found in the appendix of this book.

Homily

After the reading, the celebrant gives a short homily, explaining to those present the significance of what has been read. His purpose will be to lead them to a deeper understanding of the mystery of baptism and to encourage the parents and godparents to a ready acceptance of the responsibilities that arise from the sacrament.

After the homily, or in the course of or after the litany, it is desirable to have a period of silence while all pray at the invitation of the celebrant. If convenient, a suitable song follows.

AT THE AMBO

The Liturgy of the Word

Readings and Homily

During this part of the celebration we are invited to sit and listen to the Word of God, which nourishes us on our journey of faith.

You may be asked to choose one of the four gospel readings from the facing page and one other reading from the Old or New Testament. These readings can be found in the appendix of this book. A member of your family may be invited to proclaim these readings at the baptism. The person chosen to read must be one who is comfortable with proclaiming the Word of God both publicly and with belief.

Every family has its own set of stories that are told and retold every time they gather. As you plan your baby's baptism you are beginning a new chapter in your family's story, one that is inextricably interwoven with God's story. The telling of stories is so important in the Christian family that every time we gather to celebrate a sacrament we are invited to listen to the story of God's love for us. We call this part of the celebration The Liturgy of the Word. The readings for baptism are specially chosen to help us better understand the significance and meaning of this sacrament.

Intercessions and Litany

Then the intercessions (Prayer of the Faithful) are said:

Celebrant   My brothers and sisters, let us ask our Lord Jesus
             Christ to look lovingly on these children who are to
             be baptised, on their parents and godparents, and on
             all the baptised.

Reader: By the mystery of your death and resurrection, bathe
             these children in light, give them the new life of
             baptism and welcome them into your holy Church.
             (We pray)
R: Lord, hear our prayer.

Reader: Through baptism and confirmation make them your
             faithful followers and witnesses to your gospel.
             (We pray)
R: Lord, hear our prayer.

Reader: Lead them by holy life to the joys of God's kingdom.
             (We pray)
R: Lord, hear our prayer.

Reader: Make the lives of their parents and godparents
             examples of faith to inspire these children. (We pray)
R: Lord, hear our prayer.

Reader: Keep their families always in your love. (We pray)
R: Lord, hear our prayer.

Reader: Renew the grace of our baptism in each one of us.
             (We pray)
R: Lord, hear our prayer.

Intercessions and Litany

During this part of the celebration we are invited to bring our prayers to God. You might be invited to write some of the Intercessions. You can include prayers for relatives and friends who have died or who cannot be with you on this special occasion. Keep these prayers short and simple. It is good practice to show them to the priest or baptismal team member who is helping you to prepare the ceremony. Invite someone from your family to read the prayers at the baptism.

If we want to keep our relationships strong we need to spend time with the people we care about. The same is true of our relationship with God. We need to make time for God in our lives and one of the ways that we can do this is through prayer. We can pray in many different ways and in many different places. We can light a candle and spend some time in quiet prayer. We pray as a community every time we come together at Mass. Praying with your child at home is an important part of being a Christian family. Children love to pray and they will cherish the time that you spend with them teaching them some of the simple prayers of our faith and praying with them. You can also encourage them to give thanks for all that they have and ask God's blessing on those they love. Family traditions of saying a prayer at bedtime or a prayer of thanks before meals can be created. We have included these prayers in the chapter 'The Journey Continues'.

The celebrant next invites all present to invoke the saints.

Holy Mary, Mother of God	pray for us
Saint John the Baptist	pray for us
Saint Joseph	pray for us
Saint Peter and Saint Paul	pray for us

The names of other saints may be added, especially the patrons of the children to be baptised, and of the church or locality.
The litany concludes

All holy men and women   pray for us

During this part of the celebration we ask the saints to pray for us and with us as we begin our journey of faith with this child. If members of the family or godparents are called after saints ask the priest to include these names in the litany. Consider including the name of the saint whose feast day is closest to your child's birth date in their names. You can find this information by going to www.catholic.org/saints.

When we ask the saints to pray for and with us we are reminded that their stories are an important part of our Christian story. The saints gave their lives to God in a very special way. Their stories help us on our journey of faith and give us strength and encouragement to live as Christians.

Not all of us can be saints, but our baptism calls us to be members of God's family in a special way. Our baptism is both an invitation and a challenge to live our lives according to the gospel, to do what Jesus asks of us, to love one another as Jesus loved us. This is no easy task but we are not alone on our journey. We are helped on our way by all the baptised and we can look to the lives of the saints for inspiration and courage.

PREPARATORY RITES

Prayer of Exorcism
After the invocations, the celebrant says

A   Almighty and ever-living God,
    you sent your only Son into the world
    to cast out the power of Satan, spirit of evil,
    to deliver us from the kingdom of darkness,
    and bring us into the splendour of your kingdom of light.
    We pray for these children:
    set them free from original sin,
    make them temples of your glory,
    and send your Holy Spirit to dwell within them.
    (We ask this) through Christ our Lord.

R   Amen

Anointing before Baptism
The celebrant continues:

We anoint you with the oil of salvation
in the name of Christ our Saviour;
may he strengthen you with his power,
who lives and reigns for ever and ever.

R   Amen

He anoints each child on the breast with the oil of catechumens.

Preparatory Rites

Prayer of Exorcism
During this part of the celebration we pray that your child will always be guided and protected by God.

The word 'exorcism' is one that brings to mind all kinds of images not normally connected with a joyful celebration such as baptism and it may seem strange that the baptism ceremony includes such a prayer. On one level this prayer highlights the many temptations offered by the world in which we live. We know that we are constantly being tempted to turn away from the way of light and love offered by God and to be selfish and careless in our dealings with one another. But on a more profound level this prayer is a powerful reminder that God's love can conquer all evil. A parent's first instinct is to keep their child safe. But you know that as they grow they will be confronted by the temptations of the world.

So at this point of the ceremony we now pray that your child will always be graced with God's strength and guidance on their journey through life. We pray too, that God's Holy Spirit given to us in baptism will help this child remain strong and faithful to God's love in their lives.

Anointing before Baptism
This prayer of anointing asks that your child will be strengthened by God as they begin their new life in Christ.

This is the first of the two anointings with oil of your child during the baptism ceremony. The oil used in this anointing, called the oil of catechumens, is blessed olive oil. 'Catechumen' is the name given to a person who is preparing to become a member of the Church.

Oil was very important in the world of the Old Testament. To have enough corn, wine and oil was seen as a sign of God's blessing. The early Christians used oil for many things, cooking, giving light and washing and protecting the skin.

The celebrant will ask you to loosen your child's robe and will then rub the oil of catechumens on your child's chest. This is a gesture of care and protection, just as you rub oils and cream on your baby's skin to protect and care for it. This gesture of anointing can also act as a reminder that we are all called, as members of the Christian community, to care for and support each other on our journey of faith. We pray that your child will be strengthened and protected through the power of Christ's love.

AT THE FONT

Celebration of Baptism

Invitation to Prayer

When they come to the font, the celebrant briefly reminds the congregation of the wonderful work of God whose plan is to sanctify humankind, body and soul, through water.

My dear brothers and sisters, we now ask God to give these children new life in abundance through water and the Holy Spirit.

AT THE FONT

Celebration of Baptism

Invitation to Prayer
Parents and godparents are now invited to bring the children to the baptismal font.

The time has now arrived for the actual baptism of your child. The font is only used to welcome new members. Just as Jesus went down into the waters of the Jordan and heard God say 'This is my beloved on whom my favour rests', so now you bring your child to the waters of the font to celebrate their being a beloved child of God.

The early generations of Christians (who were typically baptised as adults) were baptised by being plunged into whatever body of water was available or water was simply poured over their heads as they professed their faith. As time progressed the custom of blessing the water began to appear.

Prayer over the Water

Then turning to the font he says one of the following blessings:

Father, you give us grace through sacramental signs, which tell us of the wonders of your unseen power.
In baptism we use your gift of water, which you have made a rich symbol of the grace you give us in this sacrament.
At the very dawn of creation your Spirit breathed on the waters, making them the wellsprings of all holiness.
The waters of the great flood you made a sign of the waters of baptism that make an end of sin and a new beginning of goodness.
Through the waters of the Red Sea you led Israel out of slavery to be an image of God's holy people, set free from sin by baptism.
In the waters of the Jordan your Son was baptised by John and anointed with the Spirit.
Your Son willed that water and blood should flow from his side as he hung upon the cross.
After his resurrection he told his disciples: 'Go out and teach all nations, baptising them in the name of the Father, and of the Son, and of the Holy Spirit.'
Father, look now with love upon your Church and unseal for it the fountain of baptism.
By the power of the Holy Spirit give to this water the grace of your Son, so that in the Sacrament of Baptism all those whom you have created in your likeness may be cleansed from sin and rise to a new birth of innocence by water and the Holy Spirit.

The celebrant touches the water with his right hand and continues:

We ask you, Father, with your Son to send the Holy Spirit upon the waters of this font. May all who are buried with Christ in the death of baptism rise also with him to newness of life. We ask this through Christ our Lord.

R. Amen.

Prayer over the Water

During this part of the rite the water that will be used for baptism is blessed by the priest.

We have already said that the Rite of Baptism is a rich tapestry of signs, prayers, word and gestures. In this prayer over the water we draw on all of these elements to begin to grasp the depths of God's power at work in our human story. In the course of this prayer we connect with the great moments of salvation history associated with God's use of water – the waters at the dawn of creation, the great flood, the exodus through the Red Sea, the baptism of Jesus in the Jordan, the water that flowed from the side of the crucified Christ. All these are powerful moments of God's saving intervention in the human story.

The prayer begins by reminding us that God communicates to us through signs. In the sacraments of the Church God gives us visible signs (water, bread, wine, oil) so that we might begin to recognise and welcome the many ways in which we are loved by God and in which we receive God's grace. In the sacrament of Baptism we can begin to tell ourselves some of what God's love is like.

Together, water and prayer point to a God who:

> calls us to be a new creation,
> calls us to a life of holiness,
> forgives our sins,
> frees us from the many slaveries of the world,
> gifts us with the spirit,
> calls us to be generous in sharing this good news with others,
> has created us in God's own likeness, and
> calls us to share in Christ's resurrection.

Profession of Faith
The celebrant speaks to the parents and godparents these words:

Dear parent and godparents:
You have come here to present these children for baptism. By water and the Holy Spirit they are to receive the gift of new life from God, who is love.

On your part, you must make it your constant care to bring them up in the practice of their faith. See that the divine life which God gives them is kept safe from the poison of sin, to grow always stronger in their hearts.

If your faith makes you ready to accept this responsibility, renew now the vows of your own baptism. Reject sin; profess our faith in Christ Jesus. This is the faith of the Church. This is the faith in which these children are about to be baptised.

Renunciation of Sin
The celebrant questions the parents and godparents:

Celebrant
Do you reject Satan?

Parents and godparents
I do.

Celebrant
And all his works?

Parents and godparents
I do.

Celebrant
And all his empty promises?

Parents and godparents
I do.

Profession of Faith

As a parent, there are many things that you need to do in order to ensure that your child grows physically, emotionally and mentally. As a Christian parent you will also need to help your child to grow in faith. At this stage of the Rite of Baptism you are reminded once more of this responsibility.

The sacraments are not magic. The sacraments presume faith and faith presumes an ongoing and growing relationship with God. Your child will need your guidance, example and care in order for the faith celebrated in their baptism to grow and flourish. This faith finds expression in a prayer life but also in the values that guide a family as they live and grow together.

In the Sacrament of Baptism the child is baptised into the faith of the Christian community and the faith of the parents. It is this faith that is professed now and that you will share with your child. When a parent has faith, the natural instinct is to want to share that faith. If we believe that something is inherently good we want to share it with our children.

To this end, we don't wait until they are adults to let our children decide whether or not to eat vegetables. We allow them to explore food, we expose them to the richness of what is out there and we persist in sharing with them what is good – very often building on our own repertoire of food unexpectedly. So it is with faith. Hopefully as a parent you will take the opportunity to share with your children the richness of your faith, exposing them to its many dimensions and perhaps in turn you will find your own faith life enriched.

Renunciation of Sin

The profession of faith is preceded by the renunciation of sin.

The renunciation of sin highlights that when we turn to God there implies a turning away from evil. When we talk about the new life that baptism continually calls us to, there is of necessity an old life that we are shedding.

Faith calls each one of us to make choices in our lives and to take Christ as our role model. In the renunciation of sin, as adult members of the Church you are being invited to actively and consciously turn away from what is evil in the world and to live and be guided by the values and principles of Christ.

Profession of Faith

Next the celebrant asks for the threefold profession of faith from the parents and godparents:

Celebrant

Do you believe in God, the Father almighty, creator of heaven and earth?

Parents and godparents

I do.

Celebrant

Do you believe in Jesus Christ, his only Son, our Lord, who was born of the Virgin Mary, was crucified, died and was buried, rose from the dead, and is now seated at the right hand of the Father?

Parents and godparents

I do.

Celebrant

Do you believe in the Holy Spirit, the holy Catholic Church, the communion of saints, the forgiveness of sins, the resurrection of the body and life everlasting?

Parents and godparents

I do.

The celebrant and the congregation give their assent to this profession of faith:

Celebrant

This is our faith. This is the faith of the Church. We are proud to profess it, in Christ Jesus our Lord.

R. Amen.

Profession of Faith
Parents and godparents are asked to profess their belief before the baptism of the children.

The profession of faith reminds us of the belief that unites us as Christians. This statement of faith contains the central elements of our Christian faith. So important are these beliefs that we are invited annually to renew our commitment to them at the Easter Vigil. The beliefs professed here are a core part of our identity as baptised Christians.

So when you bring your child for baptism, together with all the parents and godparents present, you are asked to once more profess your belief in these faith statements – the faith in which your child will be baptised.

The response to the questions is a statement of the individual – 'I do'. This is your opportunity to claim these statements of faith for yourself. At the end of the profession the celebrant proclaims: 'This is our faith. This is the faith of the Church.' The faith that you have claimed for yourself is a faith you share with the Christian family. It is a faith that your child will continue to grow into as a member of this Christian family. In the future they will stand with the Christian community and make this profession for themselves in Confirmation and at the Easter Vigil.

Baptism
The celebrant invites the first of the families to the font. Using the name of the individual child, he questions the parents and godparents.

Celebrant
Is it your will that N. should be baptised in the faith of the Church, which we have all professed with you?

Parents and godparents
It is.

He baptises the child, saying
N., I baptise you in the name of the Father,

He immerses the child or pours water upon it.
and of the Son,

He immerses the child or pours water upon it a second time.
and of the Holy Spirit.

He immerses the child or pours water upon it a third time.
He asks the same question and performs the same action for each child.

Baptism

We now come to the high point of the Rite of Baptism – the actual baptism of your child in water, in the name of the Trinity – Father, Son and Holy Spirit.

There is something very simple about this gesture of pouring water over the head of your child. Water is part of our everyday life. We wash ourselves clean in it, we drink it to quench our thirst, we give out about it when it rains too much and we look for it in times of drought. We are more and more aware of its power to create and its power to destroy.

The many ways in which we use water can help us in part to understand what is happening in baptism. In this sacrament we take water and use it in such a way that it now carries all the above meanings and more.

When you bring your child to the font and hold them gently in your arms over the water, you welcome these waters over their head. You are also welcoming the promise these waters hold for your child and the Christian community.

This is the life-giving sacrament, the water of life that:
• washes us clean from the sin of the human condition,
• leads us to a new life in relationship with God and the Christian community.

This is the water:
• in which we drown to our old way of being and emerge as new people,
• in which we can physically feel the sweet refreshment of Christ upon us.

This is a new beginning:
• and as a beginning it celebrates what we might become as we grow in faith.

To be baptised in the name of the Trinity – in the name of the Father, Son and Holy Spirit – is to be drawn into a new set of relationships. In the months and years to come you will see the different relationships your child has with siblings, parents and grandparents grow and change. Hopefully you will also see your child's relationship with God grow and mature.

EXPLANATORY RITES

Anointing after Baptism

Then the celebrant says

God the Father of our Lord Jesus Christ
has freed you from sin,
given you a new birth by water and the Holy Spirit
and welcomed you into his holy people.
He now anoints you with the chrism of salvation.
As Christ was anointed Priest, Prophet and King,
so may you live always as members of his body,
sharing everlasting life.

R   Amen

The celebrant anoints each child on the crown of the head with
chrism, in silence.

Explanatory Rites

Anointing after Baptism

During this part of the celebration we are reminded that through our baptism we are called to be active members of our Christian community.

This is the second of the two anointings that we mentioned earlier. This time the olive oil is perfumed with balsam. Perfumed oil was very precious in Old Testament times and it was used on special occasions, such as the anointing of priests, prophets and kings, those chosen by God to lead God's people. The word 'Christ' means 'anointed one' and thus when those who followed Jesus recognised him as the Messiah, the one sent from God, they began to call him 'Christ'.

The early Christians incorporated anointing into their rite of initiation, when people wanted to become members of their community of faith. The anointing with the perfumed chrism oil was then seen as a confirmation of the baptism with water and was a real reminder of the presence of the Holy Spirit. We continue this tradition of anointing in our baptismal celebrations today. The chrism oil is used again in the celebration of the sacraments of Confirmation and Ordination.

At this time of the baptism ceremony your child will be anointed, by the priest, on the head with the perfumed oil of chrism. For many hours after baptism you and all who hold your child will see and smell this very visible sign of their membership of the body of Christ. Just as the oil is absorbed by your baby's skin, so they become absorbed into the Christian family. Through baptism your child is joined more closely with Jesus Christ and is called to share in his work as priest when they pray, prophet when they share the good news and king as they serve one another.

Clothing with White Garment
The celebrant says

N. & N. you have been given a new creation,
and have clothed yourselves in Christ.
See in this white garment
the outward sign of your Christian dignity.
With your family and friends to help you by word
and example,
bring that dignity into the everlasting life of heaven.

R. Amen.

The white garments are put on the children.

THE RITE

Clothing with white garment

The putting on of the white garment is a visible sign of the new life in Christ Jesus that you have chosen for your child.

The putting on of the white garment was a rich symbolic action of the early Church. At that time baptism was by immersion. This meant that those being baptised took off their old clothes and entered the baptismal pool where they were completely immersed in the water three times, in the name of the Father, Son and Holy Spirit. (Remember Jesus' baptism in the River Jordan.) Then they walked out of the pool and were wrapped in a new white robe. They wore this for the rest of the ceremony and often for many days afterwards. The symbol was clear, the old clothes and old way of life were left behind and a new life was begun in Christ Jesus. The white garment was the outward sign of this new life.

As noted, today most babies are brought to the church in their white baptismal clothes. However, it may be possible to retrieve some of the wonder of the clothing with the white garment. Some parishes suggest that the child be wrapped in a coloured blanket or shawl until this moment of the ceremony. They are then revealed in all their beauty. It is also possible to dress your child in a simple one piece until this point in the ceremony and then slip the white robe over their head and show them as a new creation to all those gathered.

The prayer that accompanies this part of the ceremony also reminds all those present of the responsibility to help this child on their journey of faith by their word and example.

Lighting of Candle
The celebrant takes the Easter candle and says

Receive the light of Christ

Someone from each family lights the child's candle from the Easter candle. The celebrant then says:

Parents and godparents, this light is entrusted to you to be kept burning brightly. These children of yours have been enlightened by Christ. They are to walk always as children of the light. May they keep the flame of faith alive in their hearts. When the Lord comes, may they go out to meet him with all the saints in the heavenly kingdom.

THE RITE

Lighting of Candle
At this time your child's baptismal candle is lit from the Easter candle.

The Easter or Paschal candle is lit each year from the Paschal fire at the Easter Vigil on Holy Saturday night. This candle is a reminder that Christ is the light of the world living among us. The Paschal candle is always lighting during a baptism as we begin our journey to live in the light of the Christ and it is also lit as we make our final journey home to our heavenly Father during our funeral liturgies.

The baptismal candle is lit from the Paschal candle and you are asked to accept this light of faith on behalf of your child. It is your responsibility along with the godparents and the rest of the Christian community to keep this light of faith burning for your child. This is a job for life, but you can begin when they are very young by teaching them to make the Sign of the Cross, to bless themselves with holy water, to say simple prayers together and, most importantly, by living out your own baptismal promise to share the light of Christ in your everyday lives together.

Ephphetha
The celebrant touches the ears and mouth of each child with his thumb, saying:

The Lord Jesus made the deaf hear and the dumb speak. May he soon touch your ears to receive his word and your mouth to proclaim his faith, to the praise and glory of God the Father.

R. Amen.

Ephphetha

At this point in the celebration your child's ears and mouth are blessed by the priest. You might like to look up and read the story of how Jesus healed the man who could not hear or speak in the Gospel of Mark, chapter 7; verses 31-37.

The word 'Ephphetha' means 'be opened' and it was spoken by Jesus when he healed a man who was deaf and could not speak clearly. Mark tells us that Jesus placed his fingers in the man's ears and touched his tongue. He then looked up to heaven and said 'Ephphetha' and the man was cured.

This blessing of the ears and the mouth is the last of the rites that help us to more fully understand the meaning of baptism. It is a blessing that is an optional part of the ceremony in many countries but is usually used in the Irish Church. As the priest blesses the ears and mouth we pray that we will continue to be faithful to our baptismal mission, particularly in relation to this child, to hear God's word in our lives and to share it with others. This prayer looks forward to the day when your child will be able to hear God's word and share it with others.

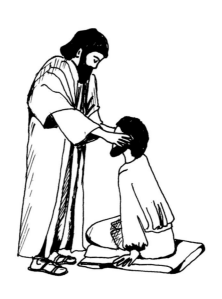

AT THE ALTAR

Concluding Rite
Next there is a procession to the altar.

The Lord's Prayer
The celebrant stands in front of the altar and addresses the parents, godparents and the whole assembly in these of similar words:

Dearly beloved, these children have been reborn in baptism. They are now called children of God, for so indeed they are. In Confirmation they will receive the fullness of God's Spirit. In Holy Communion they will share the banquet of Christ's sacrifice, calling God their Father in the midst of the Church. In their name, in the spirit of adopted children, let us pray together in the words our Lord has given us:

All present join the celebrant in singing or saying
Our Father who art in heaven, hallowed by thy name.
Thy kingdom come, thy will be done on earth as it is in heaven.
Give us this day our daily bread and forgive us our trespasses as we forgive those who trespass against us;
And lead us not into temptation but deliver us from evil.

THE RITE

AT THE ALTAR

Concluding Rite
The newly baptised, their parents and godparents gather around the altar for the Concluding Rite, during which all pray the Our Father and receive God's blessing before leaving.

Procession to the Altar
In this rite so far we have travelled from the door of the church, to the ambo and to the font. On the day of your child's baptism you may be asked at this stage of the rite to make a final journey to the altar. This journey is made because it is here the Christian community gathers to celebrate the sacrament of the Eucharist.

In the future the Church's hope is that the children who have celebrated the sacrament of Baptism will come to celebrate the sacraments of Confirmation and Eucharist. Together these three sacraments welcome new members fully into the Church.

The Concluding Rite of Baptism takes place around the altar as a sign and reminder that the journey your child is making is incomplete. It looks forward to the day when your child will share in the Bread of Life from this table.

Our Father
As we come to the end of our celebration of Baptism we are invited to pray the Lord's Prayer together. This is the prayer given to us by Jesus, who taught us to call God 'Father'. It is a prayer that from the very beginning held a special place in the life of the Christian community. Indeed many of the early Christian communities committed themselves to praying it three times every day.

In a world of growing virtual relationships, the Lord's Prayer is a powerful reminder that God wants a real relationship with us. God, our Father, wants our daily conversation of life and prayer.

In a world of seemingly instant gratification, coupled with growing despair, this prayer tells the truth that our deepest hunger can only be satisfied by God – who is our daily bread.

In a world in which we hear daily of the destructive nature of war, intolerance and violence this prayer calls us to forgive.

In a world of so many different messages and attractions this prayer places our trust and confidence in the path to which God calls us.

Blessing and dismissal

The celebrant first blesses the mothers, who hold the children in their arms, then the father and lastly the entire assembly.

Celebrant

God the father, through his Son, the Virgin Mary's child, has brought joy to all Christian mothers, as they see the hope of eternal life shine on their children.
May he bless the mothers of these children.
They now thank God for the gift of their children.
May they be one with them in thanking God for ever in heaven, in Christ Jesus, our Lord.
R. Amen.

Celebrant

God is the giver of all life, human and divine.
May he bless the fathers of these children.
With their wives they will be the first teachers of their children in the ways of faith.
May they also be the best of teachers, bearing witness to the faith by what they say and do, in Christ Jesus, our Lord.
R. Amen.

Celebrant

By God's gift, through water and the Holy Spirit, we are reborn to everlasting life.
In his goodness, may he continue to pour out his blessings upon all present,
Who are his sons and daughters.
May he make them always, wherever they may be, faithful members of his holy people.
May he send his peace upon all who are gathered here, in Christ Jesus, our Lord.
R. Amen.

Celebrant

Go in peace.
R. Thanks be to God.

Blessing and Dismissal

In every liturgical rite we conclude our time in prayer by seeking God's blessing on those who have gathered. It reminds us that it is God who acts in the liturgy. It reminds us that God is the ultimate source of the blessings in our lives. It reminds us that we are people of faith who believe that God does indeed love us.

In the rite of baptism the mothers of the children are first blessed in a prayer that recognises the joy of motherhood and that acknowledges their children as gifts from God.

The prayer for fathers reminds both mothers and fathers of the reality that faith will be taught (or caught!) in the home. As parents it is you who are the first teachers and hopefully you will be the best. This prayer reminds us that we teach by word and action.

The blessing prayer then widens to include all who have gathered to celebrate this sacrament. It is a prayer that invites all present to welcome God's blessings into their lives and to live as faithful members of the Christian community. The final part of the prayer is a prayer for peace – the peace that is beyond all human understanding and that can come from God alone.

It is in this Spirit of peace that you will be invited to depart – to bring peace to your homes and to your lives; what greater gift can you hope to bring as you leave the church with its newest member in your arms!

THE JOURNEY CONTINUES

Once the baptism celebration is over the journey of helping your child grow in their faith continues. This may seem a daunting task but there are some very simple things that you can do with your child to ensure that the light of faith keeps burning brightly in your family. In the following pages we offer some suggestions that might help you with this important work.

Memories
The memories of baptism are very special but they will fade with time so it might be a good idea to make a 'baptism box' where you place all the keepsakes of the day; photos, the baptism candle, cards from family and friends, a copy of the Rite of Baptism, the baptismal certificate when you receive it and any other mementoes that you want to keep safely. You might like to write something about the day for your child to read in later years. Write your child's name on the box with the date and place of the baptism and put it somewhere that you will be able to access it in years to come when your child wants to know about their baptism. This box could be brought out on the anniversary of your child's baptism each year and added to as the other sacraments of initiation are celebrated.

Anniversary of Baptism
We celebrate all kinds of anniversaries in families but how many of us remember and celebrate the anniversary of our

baptism? Most people are unaware of the date of their baptism. Why not begin a tradition of a simple celebration of your child's baptism on the anniversary each year? It might take place as you gather round the table to have dinner. The following is a suggestion of the form that the ritual might take.

Place your child's baptismal candle and a bowl of water on the table. Invite someone to light the baptismal candle:

Leader   On the day of (your child's name's) baptism we lit this candle from the Easter Candle in the church. We promised to keep the light of faith burning for you. Today we light this candle again to show that we are all doing our best to keep that promise.

On the day of (your child's name's) baptism, you were welcomed into the church. We gave you a name and marked you with sign of the cross. Today we ask everyone to trace the sign of the cross on (your child's name's) forehead as we remember that you are a follower of Jesus Christ.

When this is finished:

Leader   I now invite everyone to dip their finger in the water and trace the sign of the cross on their own forehead as a reminder that each one of us became a follower of Christ through our own baptism.

As we begin our meal we ask God's blessing on the food that we are about to eat, on all of us and especially on those who have very little to eat today. We pray together:

Bless us, O God, as we sit together.
Bless the food we eat today.

Bless the hands that made the food.
Bless us, O God.
Amen

Family Bible
The stories that are important to us as God's family are written down in the Bible. Many families have a Bible that has been handed down from generation to generation. If your family doesn't have a Bible perhaps you can buy one and begin a new tradition as you prepare for your child's baptism. A lot of Family Bibles sit on a shelf and are never opened. Make sure that yours is not one of these. Read Bible stories to your children the same way that you read other stories. This is a great way to learn more about your faith.

Suggestions for Family Bible:
Contemporary English Version, Children's Illustrated Edition
ISBN 978 1 58516 076 1

Praying Together
Creating opportunities to pray with your child is a very important part of helping them to grow in their faith and build a relationship with their God. You can pray together as a family in many different ways and in many different places.

Morning Prayer
In most houses mornings are very busy times and prayer is often the last thing on our minds as we hurry to get to work, school or crèches. Some parishes give families holy water to bring home on the day of baptism. This holy water can serve to remind us of our baptism. The water font at the door of a church is also a reminder of baptism. By placing a holy water font by the door to your home you and your family can have a daily reminder of baptism – while also making a link between your home and the local church community. Encourage each member of the family to bless themselves as they leave the house

in the morning. This simple gesture invokes God's blessing on all as they begin their day.

Mealtimes
Sitting down to eat together used to be part and parcel of family life. Mealtimes were an opportunity to catch up and find out about what had happened during the day. In some families this is still very much the norm, but for many, different work practices, after school activities, long commutes and many other factors mean that often mealtimes are staggered. Therefore, the times when we do get the chance to sit down together as a family are precious. On these occasions a blessing prayer, Prayer before Meals, might be used before you begin to eat.

Night Prayer
Lighting a candle at the beginning of your prayer together can create a special atmosphere, a visible reminder of God's presence among us. This might be done just before bedtime when you spend a few minutes looking back over the day, giving thanks for all the good things that have happened, asking forgiveness for the times when we hurt ourselves or others and asking God to care for the people or situations in our lives that give us cause for concern. These are precious moments which both you and your child will come to value and cherish.

Common Prayers
Sign of the Cross
In the name of the Father,
and of the Son,
and of the Holy Spirit.
Amen.

Morning Prayer
Father in heaven, you love me,
You're with me night and day.
I want to love you always
In all I do and say.
I'll try to please you, Father.
Bless me through the day. Amen.

Night Prayer
God, our Father, I come to say
Thank you for your love today.
Thank you for my family,
And all the friends you give to me.
Guard me in the dark of night,
And in the morning send your light. Amen.

Grace Before Meals
Bless us, O God, as we sit together.
Bless the food we eat today.
Bless the hands that made the food.
Bless us, O God. Amen.

Grace After Meals
Thank you, God, for the food we have eaten.
Thank you, God, for all our friends.
Thank you, God, for everything.
Thank you, God. Amen.

Hail Mary
Hail Mary, full of grace,
The Lord is with thee.
Blessed art thou among women
And blessed is the fruit of thy womb, Jesus.
Holy Mary, mother of God,
Pray for us sinners,
Now, and at the hour of our death. Amen.

Glory be to the Father
Glory be to the Father,
And to the Son,
And to the Holy Spirit;
As it was in the beginning,
Is now and ever shall be,
World without end. Amen.

Our Father
Our Father who art in heaven
Hallowed be thy name.
Thy kingdom come,
Thy will be done
On earth as it is in heaven.
Give us this day our daily bread
And forgive us our trespasses
As we forgive those who trespass against us.
And lead us not into temptation
But deliver us from evil. Amen.

Prayer to Guardian Angel
O Angel of God, my guardian dear,
To whom God's love commits me here,
Ever this day, be at my side,
To light and guard, rule and guide. Amen.

Seasonal Prayer
The church year offers many opportunities around which you can build a tradition of prayer with your family. The following are only some of the ways in which the rhythm of the Church Year might be followed:

Advent
The Church Year begins in Advent and marking this season is a way of preparing to welcome the Christ-child at Christmas. In a world where all too often we get caught up in the hustle and

bustle of present buying, decorating and partying it is important to focus on what we are really celebrating. The lighting of the candles in sequence each week to mark the journey from Advent to Christmas will make a memory that you and your family will hold long after Christmas is over. Advent calendars have become very popular and are a great way of helping children to get a sense of the journey to Christmas. Try to find one with a religious theme to remind your child of the true meaning of the season. Put up a crib in the week before Christmas. You might like to place the figures in different places around the house and encourage your child to move them each day as they, like Mary and Joseph, journey towards Bethlehem. Put the figure of the baby Jesus in the crib on Christmas Eve and say a prayer together as a family.

Prayer: Blessing of the Advent Wreath
We pray that the richness of God's blessing may rest upon this Advent wreath, upon our home, and upon each of us, as we light our first candle in the name of the Father, and of the Son, and of the Holy Spirit. Amen

Prayer: Blessing of the Crib
We praise and thank you, O God, for the coming of Jesus.
Bless this crib and bless each one of us.
Help us to remember that we must share Jesus' light and love with those we meet.
May we always be thankful for all the gifts you have given us.
We make this prayer through Christ our Lord.
Amen.

Lent
The pillars of Lent are prayer, fasting and almsgiving. Each of these pillars suggests ways in which we can see Lent as a time to prepare for Easter. Encourage your family to see Lent as a time for doing something together to make the world in which we live a better place. The annual Trócaire Campaign is one

way in which we are helped to do this. Your family may think of others.

Easter

Easter is the high point of the Church Year, the time when we, as a community of believers, over three days celebrate the life, death and resurrection of Jesus. Make your family's participation in the Holy Week Celebrations a priority. There is no greater opportunity to come to know and understand the story of our faith.

Community Prayer

As you bring your child to be baptised, this can be an opportunity to reflect on your own connection with the Church. The Church is stronger for the participation of all its members. As a family, now and in the years ahead, you have something to bring to the life of your local parish that nobody else can substitute. What is that/what will that be?

We pray as a community every time we come together at Mass and this is central to who we are as members of the Church. There are many key moments during the Church year when our churches are packed, Christmas, Ash Wednesday, Good Friday, and Easter Sunday among others. If you are to keep the light of faith burning for your child it is important that they learn what it means to really belong to the faith community that gathers every Sunday. They need to be part of that community, to be present when they gather, to become familiar with the prayers and rituals of the Church.

As your child continues on their journey of faith there will be other sacramental occasions to prepare for and celebrate, First Penance, First Communion and Confirmation. Many parishes have programmes of preparation that encourage the active involvement of parents. Make sure that you get involved. These times are all opportunities to revisit the promises made at baptism and perhaps make a renewed effort to keep that light of faith burning.

In the words of Brendan Kennelly's poem 'Begin'

Every beginning is a promise born in light
Though we live in a world that dreams of ending
that always seems about to give in
something that will not acknowledge conclusion
insists that we forever begin.

A WORD FOR GODPARENTS

It is a huge honour and privilege to be asked to be a godparent to a child. Being a godparent puts you in a particular relationship with this child – a connection now exists between the two of you that cannot be taken away. And that is a tremendous gift.

You may be wondering what is the role of a godparent? What are you expected to do? Is there a job description?

The primary role of a godparent is one of support. At the very beginning of the ceremony of baptism you are asked: "Are you ready to help these parents in their duty as Christian mothers and fathers?" This is what is being asked of you. This is your job description. The support is in the context of mothers and fathers handing on the Christian faith.

As friends or family members there is no doubt but that you will want to support these parents. But the question you are being asked in the ceremony of baptism is whether you are ready to help them in raising their child in the Christian faith. This is a question that you may need to ponder. It is an opportunity for you to reflect on whether you are in a position to offer this kind of support.

How can you show this support? On the day of baptism it can be expressed by your participation in the ceremony itself. There are definite things you will be asked to do during the ceremony. For example, you will be invited to sign the child on the forehead with the sign of the cross at the beginning of the ceremony. There are questions that will be asked of you during the ceremony and you will be asked to come to the baptismal font at the time of baptism in solidarity with the parents. Your engagement in all these questions and actions will itself offer support to parents.

In the days and years after the baptism there will be ample opportunities to show your support – birthdays, anniversaries of baptisms, first communion days, confirmation … On these days you might consider the gift of time you can give to your godchild. Your presence at significant religious events in their life will underscore the importance of these occasions.

Outside of these events, you can encourage and help nurture the child's emerging faith through your conversations and time spent with them.

You might also consider the physical gifts you give your godchild. There may be opportunities to give your godchild gifts such as a bible, a cross, religious images, music, DVD's and books that reflect the Christian faith.

But the greatest gift you can give is the gift of your example and love – a love that makes the Christian life visible.

APPENDIX
READINGS FOR THE
BAPTISM OF INFANTS

Readings are presented in pairings. These are suggestions only.
Any other suitable pairing may be used.

FIRST READING FROM THE OLD TESTAMENT

1

A READING FROM THE BOOK OF EXODUS (17:3-7)

Give us water to drink.

Tormented by thirst, the people complained against Moses. 'Why did you bring us out of Egypt?' they said. 'Was it so that I should die of thirst, my children too, and my cattle?' Moses appealed to the Lord. 'How am I to deal with this people? He said. 'A little more and they will stone me!' The Lord said to Moses, 'Take with you some of the elders of Israel and move on to the forefront of the people; take in your hand the staff with which you struck the river, and go. I shall be standing before you there on the rock, at Horeb. You must strike the rock, and water will flow from it for the people to drink.' This is what Moses did, in the sight of the elders of Israel. The place was named Massah and Meribah because of the grumbling of the sons of Israel and because they put the Lord to the test by saying, 'Is the Lord with us, or not?'.

This is the word of the Lord.

RESPONSORIAL PSALM (Ps 22.Rv.1)

R The Lord is my shepherd;
there is nothing I shall want.

1. The Lord is my shepherd;
there is nothing I shall want.
Fresh and green are the pastures
where he gives me repose.
Near restful waters he leads me,
to revive my drooping spirit. R

2. He guides me along the right path;
he is true to his name.
If I should walk in the valley of darkness
no evil would I fear.
You are there with your crook and staff;
with these you give me comfort. R

3. You have prepared a banquet for me
in the sight of my foes.
My head you have anointed with oil;
my cup is overflowing. R

4. Surely goodness and kindness shall follow me
all the days of my life.
In the lord's own house shall I dwell
for ever and ever. R

2

A READING FROM THE PROPHET EZEKIEL (36:24-28)

I shall pour clean water over you, and you will be cleansed of all your defilement.

The Lord says this: I am going to take you from among the nations and gather you together from all the foreign countries, and bring you home to your own land. I shall pour clean water over you and you will be cleansed; I shall cleanse you of all your defilement and all your idols. I shall give you a new heart, and put a new spirit in you; I shall remove the heart of stone from your bodies and give you a heart of flesh instead. I shall put my spirit in you, and make you keep my laws and sincerely respect my observances. You will live in the land which I gave your ancestors. You shall be my people and I will be your God.

This is the word of the Lord.

RESPONSORIAL PSALM (Ps33:2-3. 6-9. 14-19. R v6. Alt. Rv.9)

> R Look towards the Lord and be radiant.
> or
> R Taste and see that the Lord is good.

1. I will bless the Lord at all times,
   his praise always on my lips;
   in the Lord my soul shall make its boast,
   the humble shall hear and be glad. R

2. Look towards him and be radiant;
   Let your faces not be abashed.
   This poor man called; the Lord heard him
   and rescued him from all his distress R

3. The angel of the Lord is encamped
   around those who revere him, to rescue them.
   Taste and see that the Lord is good.
   He is happy who seeks refuge in him. R

4. Then keep your tongue from evil
   and your lips from speaking deceit.
   Turn aside from evil and do good;
   seek and strive after peace. R

5. The lord turns his face against the wicked
   to destroy their remembrance from the earth.
   The Lord turns his eyes to the just
   and his ears to their appeal. R

6. They call and the Lord hears
   and rescues them in all their distress.
   The lord is close to the broken–hearted;
   those whose spirit is crushed he will save. R

3

A READING FROM THE PROPHET EZEKIEL (47:1-9.12)

I saw a stream of water coming from the Temple, bringing life to all wherever it flowed.

The angel brought me to the entrance of the Temple, where a stream came out from under the Temple threshold and flowed eastwards, since the Temple faced east. The water flowed from under the right side of the Temple, south of the altar. He took me out by the north gate and led me right round outside as far as the outer east gate where the water flowed out of the right-hand side. The man went to the east holding his measuring line and measured off a thousand cubits; he them made me wade across the stream; the water reached my ankles. He measured off another thousand and made me wade across the stream again; the water reached my knees. He measured off another thousand and made me wade across again; the water reached my waist. He measured off another thousand; it was now a river which I could not cross; the stream had swollen and was now deep water, a river impossible to cross. He then said, 'Do you see, son of man?' He took me further, then brought me back to the bank of the river. When I got back, there were many trees on each bank of the river. He said, 'This water flows east down to the Arabah and to the sea; and flowing into the sea it makes its waters wholesome. Wherever the river flows, all living creatures teeming in it will live. Fish will be very plentiful, for wherever the water goes it brings health, and life teems wherever the river flows. Along the river, on either bank, will grow every kind of fruit tree with leaves that never wither and fruit that never fails; they will bear new fruit every month, because this water comes from the sanctuary. And their fruit will be good to eat and the leaves medicinal.'

This is the word of the Lord.

RESPONSORIAL PSALM (Ps 26 1.4.8-9. 13-14. R v.1 Alt R Eph 5:14)

> R The Lord is my light and my help.
> or
> R Wake up from your sleep,
>   rise from the dead,
>   and Christ will shine on you.

1. The Lord is my light and my help;
   whom shall I fear?
   The Lord is the stronghold of my life;
   before whom shall I shrink? R

2. There is one thing I ask of the Lord,
   for this I long,
   to live in the house of the Lord,
   all the days of my life, to savour the sweetness of the Lord,
   to behold his temple. R

3. It is your face, O Lord, that I seek;
   hide not your face.
   Dismiss not your servant in anger;
   you have been my help. R

4. I am sure I shall see the Lord's goodness
   in the land of the living.
   Hope in him, hold firm and take heart.
   Hope in the Lord! R

SECOND READING FROM THE NEW TESTAMENT

1

A READING FROM THE LETTER OF ST PAUL TO THE ROMANS (6:3-5)

When we were baptised we went into the tomb with him: let us live a new life.

When we were baptised in Christ Jesus we were baptised in his death; in other words, when we were baptised we went into the tomb with him and joined him in death, so that as Christ was raised from the dead by the Father's glory, we too might live a new life.

If in union with Christ we have imitated his death, we shall also imitate him in his resurrection.

This is the word of the Lord.

2

A READING FROM THE LETTER OF ST PAUL TO THE ROMANS (8:28-32)

To become true images of his Son.

We know that by turning everything to their good God co-operates with all those who love him, with all those that he has called according to his purpose. They are the ones he chose especially long ago and intended to become true images of his Son, so that his Son might be the eldest of many brothers. He called those he intended for this; those he called he justified, and with those he justified he shared his glory.

After saying this, what can we add? With God on our side who can be against us? Since God did not spare his own Son, but gave him up to benefit us all, we may be certain, after such a gift, that he will not refuse anything he can give.

This is the word of the Lord.

3

A READING FROM THE FIRST LETTER OF ST PAUL TO THE CORINTHIANS (12:12-13)

In the one Spirit we were all baptised.

Just as a human body, though it is made up of many parts, is a single unit because all these parts, though many, make one body, so it is with Christ. In the one Spirit we were all baptised, Jews as well as Greeks, slaves as well as citizens, and one Spirit was given to us all to drink.

This is the word of the Lord.

4

A READING FROM THE LETTER OF ST PAUL TO THE GALATIANS (3:26-28)

All baptised in Christ, you have all clothed yourselves in Christ.

You are, all of you, sons of God through faith in Christ Jesus. All baptised in Christ, you have all clothed yourselves in Christ, and there are no more distinctions between Jew and Greek, slave and free, male and female, but all of you are one in Christ Jesus.

This is the word of the Lord.

5

A READING FROM THE LETTER OF ST PAUL TO THE EPHESIANS (4:1-6)

One Lord, one faith, One baptism.

I, the prisoner in the Lord, implore you to lead a life worthy of your vocation. Bear with one another charitably, in complete selflessness, gentleness and patience. Do all you can to preserve the unity of the spirit by the peace that binds you together. There is one Body, one Spirit, just as you were all called into one and the same hope when you were called. There is one Lord, one faith, one baptism and one God who is Father of all, over all, through all and within all.

This is the word of the Lord.

6

A READING FROM THE FIRST LETTER OF ST PETER (2:4-5.9-10)

You are a chosen race, a royal priesthood.

Jesus Christ is the living stone, rejected by men but chosen by God and precious to him; set yourselves close to him so that you too, the holy priesthood that offers the spiritual sacrifices which he has made acceptable to God, may be living stones making a spiritual house.

You are a chosen race, a royal priesthood, a consecrated nation, a people set apart to sing the praises of God who called you out of the darkness into his wonderful light. Once you were not a people at all and now you are the People of God; once you were outside the mercy and now you have been given mercy.

This is the word of the Lord.

GOSPEL

1

GOSPEL ACCLAMATION (Jn 14:6)

Alleluia, Alleluia!
I am the Way, the Truth, and the Life, says the Lord;
no one can come to the Father except through me.
Alleluia!

A READING FROM THE HOLY GOSPEL ACCORDING TO MATTHEW (22:35-40)

This is the greatest and the first commandment.

To disconcert Jesus, one of the Pharisees, a lawyer, put a question, 'Master, which is the greatest commandment of the Law?' Jesus said, 'You must love the Lord your God with all your heart, with all your soul, and with all your mind. This is the greatest and the first commandment. The second resembles it. You must love your neighbour as yourself. On these two commandments hang the whole Law, and the Prophets also.'

This is the Gospel of the Lord.

2

GOSPEL ACCLAMATION (Eph 4:5-6)

Alleluia, alleluia!
There is one Lord, one faith, one baptism,
and one God, who is Father of all.
Alleluia!

A READING FROM THE HOLY GOSPEL ACCORDING TO MATTHEW (28:18-20)

Make disciples of all the nations, baptise them in the name of the Father and of the Son and of the Holy Spirit.

Jesus came up and spoke to his disciples. He said, 'All authority in heaven and on earth has been given to me. Go, therefore, make disciples of all the nations; baptise them in the name of the Father and of the Son and of the Holy Spirit, and teach them to observe all the commands I gave you. And know that I am with you always; yes to the end of time.'

This is the Gospel of the Lord.

3

GOSPEL ACCLAMATION (cf. 2 Tim 1:10)

Alleluia, alleluia!
Our Saviour, Christ Jesus, abolished death, and he has proclaimed life through the Good News.
Alleluia!

A READING FROM THE HOLY GOSPEL ACCORDING TO MARK (1:9-11)

He was baptised in the Jordan by John.

Jesus came from Nazareth to Galilee and was baptised in the Jordan by John. No sooner had he come up out of the water than he saw the heavens torn apart and the Spirit, like a dove, descending on him. And a voice came from heaven, 'You are my Son, the Beloved; my favour rests on you.'

This is the Gospel of the Lord.

4

GOSPEL ACCLAMATION (1 Peter 2:9)

Alleluia, alleluia!
You are a chosen race, a royal priesthood a consecrated nation; sing the praises of God who called you out of the darkness into his wonderful light.
Alleluia!

A READING FROM THE HOLY GOSPEL ACCORDING TO MARK (10:13-16)

Let the little children come to me.

People were bringing little children to Jesus, for him to touch them. The disciples turned them away, but when Jesus saw this he was indignant and said to them, 'Let the little children come to me; do not stop them; for it is to such as these that the kingdom of God belongs. I tell you solemnly, anyone who does not welcome the kingdom of God like a little child will never enter it.' Then he put his arms round them, laid his hands on them and gave them his blessing.

This is the Gospel of the Lord.

5

GOSPEL ACCLAMATION (Jn 8:12)

Alleluia, alleluia!
I am the light of the world, says the Lord;
anyone who follows me will have the light of life.
Alleluia!

A READING FROM THE HOLY GOSPEL ACCORDING TO MARK (12:28-34)

Listen, Israel, love the Lord your God with all your heart.

One of the scribes came up and put a question to Jesus, 'Which is the first of all the commandments?' Jesus replied, 'This is the first: Listen, Israel, the Lord our God is the one Lord, and you must love the Lord your God with all your heart, with all your soul, with all your mind and with all your strength. The second is this: You must love your neighbour as yourself. There is no commandment greater than these.' The scribe said to him, 'Well spoken, Master; what you have said is true: that he is one and there is no other. To love him with all your heart, with all your understanding and strength, and to love your neighbour as yourself, this is far more important than any holocaust or sacrifice.' Jesus, seeing how wisely he had spoken said, 'You are not far from the kingdom of God.' And after that no one dared to question him any more.

This is the Gospel of the Lord.

Shorter form

A READING FROM THE HOLY GOSPEL ACCORDING TO MARK (12:28-31)

Listen, Israel, love the Lord your God with all your heart.

One of the scribes came up and put a question to Jesus, 'Which is the first of all the commandments?' Jesus replied, 'This is the first: Listen, Israel, the Lord our God is the one Lord, and you must love the Lord your God with all your heart, with all your soul, with all your mind and with all your strength. The second is this: You must love your neighbour as yourself. There is no commandment greater than these.'

This is the Gospel of the Lord.

6

GOSPEL ACCLAMATION (Jn 3:16)

Alleluia, alleluia!
God loved the world so much that he gave his only Son;
everyone who believes in him
has eternal life.
Alleluia!

A READING FROM THE HOLY GOSPEL ACCORDING TO JOHN (3:1-6)

Unless a man is born from above, he cannot see the kingdom of heaven.

There was one of the Pharisees called Nicodemus, a leading Jew, who came to Jesus by night and said, 'Rabbi, we know that you are a teacher who comes from God; for no one could perform the signs that you do unless God were with him.' Jesus answered:

'I tell you solemnly;
unless a man is born from above,
he cannot see the kingdom of God.'

Nicodemus said, 'How can a grown man be born? Can he go back into his mother's womb and be born again?' Jesus replied:

'I tell you most solemnly,
unless a man is born through water and the Spirit,
he cannot enter the kingdom of God:
what is born of the flesh is flesh;
what is born of the Spirit is spirit.'

This is the Gospel of the Lord.

7

GOSPEL ACCLAMATION (Jn 8:12)

Alleluia, alleluia!
I am the light of the world, says the Lord;
anyone who follows me will have the light of life.
Alleluia!

A READING FROM THE HOLY GOSPEL ACCORDING TO JOHN (4:5-14)

A spring of water, welling up to eternal life.

Jesus came to the Samaritan town called Sychar, near the land that
Jacob gave to his son Joseph. Jacob's well is there and Jesus, tired by
the journey, sat straight down by the well. It was about the sixth hour.
When a Samaritan woman came to draw water. Jesus said to her,
'Give me a drink.' His disciples had gone into the town to buy food.
The Samaritan woman said to him, 'What? You are a Jew and you ask
me, a Samaritan, for a drink?' – Jews, in fact, do not associate with
Samaritans. Jesus replied:

'If you only knew what God is offering
and who it is that is saying to you:
Give me a drink,
you would have been the one to ask,
and he would have given you living water.'

'You have no bucket, sir,' she answered, 'and the well is deep: how
could you get this living water? Are you a greater man than our father
Jacob who gave us this well and drank from it himself with his sons
and his cattle?' Jesus replied:

'Whoever drinks this water
will get thirsty again;
but anyone who drinks the water that I shall give
will never be thirsty again:
the water that I shall give
will turn into a spring inside him, welling up to eternal life.'

This is the Gospel of the Lord.

8

GOSPEL ACCLAMATION (Jn 3:16)

Alleluia, alleluia!
God loved the world so much
that he gave his only Son;
everyone who believes in him
has eternal life.
Alleluia!

A READING FROM THE HOLY GOSPEL ACCORDING TO JOHN (6:44-47)

Everyone who believes has eternal life.

Jesus said to the crowd,

'No one can come to me
unless he is drawn by the Father who sent me,
and I will raise him up on the last day.
It is written in the prophets:
they will all be taught by God:
and to hear the teaching of the Father,
and learn from it,
is to come to me.
Not that anybody has seen the Father,
except the one who comes from God:
He has seen the Father.
I tell you solemnly,
Everybody who believes has eternal life.'

This is the Gospel of the Lord.

9

GOSPEL ACCLAMATION (Jn 3:16)

Alleluia, alleluia!
I am the light of the world, says the Lord;
anyone who follows me will have the light of life
Alleluia!

A READING FROM THE HOLY GOSPEL ACCORDING TO JOHN (7:37-39)

Fountains of living water shall flow.

Jesus cried out:

'If any man is thirsty, let him come to me!
Let the man come and drink who believes in me!'

As the scripture says: from his breast shall flow fountains of living water.
He was speaking of the Spirit which those who believed in him were to receive.

This is the Gospel of the Lord.

10

GOSPEL ACCLAMATION (Jn 8:12)

Alleluia, alleluia!
I am the light of the world, says the Lord;
anyone who follows me will have the light of life
Alleluia!

A READING FROM THE HOLY GOSPEL ACCORDING TO JOHN (9:1-7)

He went off and washed, and came away with his sight restored.

As he went along, Jesus saw a man who had been blind from birth. His disciples asked him, 'Rabbi, who sinned, this man or his parents, for him to have been born blind?' 'Neither he nor his parents sinned,' Jesus answered, 'he was born blind so that the works of God might be displayed in him.

'As long as the day lasts
I must carry out the work of the one who sent me;
the night will soon be here when no one can work.

As long as I am in the world
I am the light of the world.'

Having said this, he spat on the ground, made a paste with the spittle,
put this over the eyes of the blind man, and said to him, 'Go and wash
in the Pool of Siloam' (a name that means 'sent'). So the blind man
went off and washed himself, and came away with his sight restored.

This is the Gospel of the Lord.

11

GOSPEL ACCLAMATION (1 Peter 2:9)

Alleluia, alleluia!
You are a chosen race, a royal priesthood,
a consecrated nation;
sing the praises of God
who called you out of the darkness into his wonderful light
Alleluia!

A READING FROM THE HOLY GOSPEL ACCORDING TO JOHN (15:1-11)

Whoever remains in me, with me in him, bears fruit in plenty.

Jesus said to his disciples:

'I am the true vine,
and my Father is the vinedresser.
Every branch in me that bears no fruit
he cuts away,
and every branch that does bear fruit he prunes
to make it bear more.
You are pruned already,
by means of the word that I have spoken to you.
Make your home in me, as I make mine in you.
As a branch cannot bear fruit all by itself,
but must remain part of the vine,
neither can you unless you remain in me.

I am the vine,
you are the branches.
Whoever remains in me, with me in him,
bears fruit in plenty;
for cut off from me you can do nothing.
Anyone who does not remain in me
is like a branch that has been thrown away
– he withers;
these branches are collected and thrown on the fire,
and they are burnt.
If you remain in me
and my words remains in you,
you may ask what you will
and you shall get it.
It is to the glory of my Father that you should bear much fruit,
and then you will be my disciples.
As the Father has loved me,
so I have loved you.
Remain in my love.
If you keep my commandments
you will remain in my love,
just as I have kept my Father's commandments
and remain in his love.
I have told you this
so that my own joy may be in you
and your joy be complete.'

This is the Gospel of the Lord.

12

GOSPEL ACCLAMATION (cf 2 Tim 1:10)

Alleluia, alleluia!
Our Saviour, Christ-Jesus, abolished death,
and he has proclaimed life through the Good News.
Alleluia!

A READING FROM THE HOLY GOSPEL ACCORDING TO JOHN (19:31-35)

He pierced his side, and there came out blood and water.

It was Preparation Day, and to prevent the bodies remaining on the cross during the Sabbath – since the Sabbath was a day of special solemnity – the Jews asked Pilate to have the legs broken and the bodies taken away. Consequently the soldiers came and broke the legs of the first man who had been crucified with him and then of the other. When they came to Jesus, they found he was already dead, and so instead of breaking his legs one of the soldiers pierced his side with a lance; and immediately there came out blood and water. This is the evidence of one who saw it – trustworthy evidence, and he speaks the truth – and he gives it so that you may believe as well.

This is the Gospel of the Lord.